AF479957

LAUGHTER IN CAREGIVING

Navigating Life's Tough Moments With Humor

ISBN 979-8-3304-9250-3

Publishing by Captivate Press, by arrangement with Ingram Content Group One Ingram Blvd., La Vergne, Tennessee 37086, US.
Distributions by arrangement with Ingram Content Group One Ingram Blvd., La Vergne, Tennessee 37086, US.

Printed in the U.S.A

First Captivate Press Printing , March 2025

LAUGHTER IN CAREGIVING

Navigating Life's Tough Moments With Humor

by Mr. Ollie

GRATITUDE

The author would like to thank Amedisys home care of Pulaski, TN
and Compassus hospice care of Columbia TN.
Thank you to each and every one who worked with mom.
Your professionalism, care, warmth, compassion, kindness, and comfort
is with heartfelt appreciation. Thank you so much one and all.

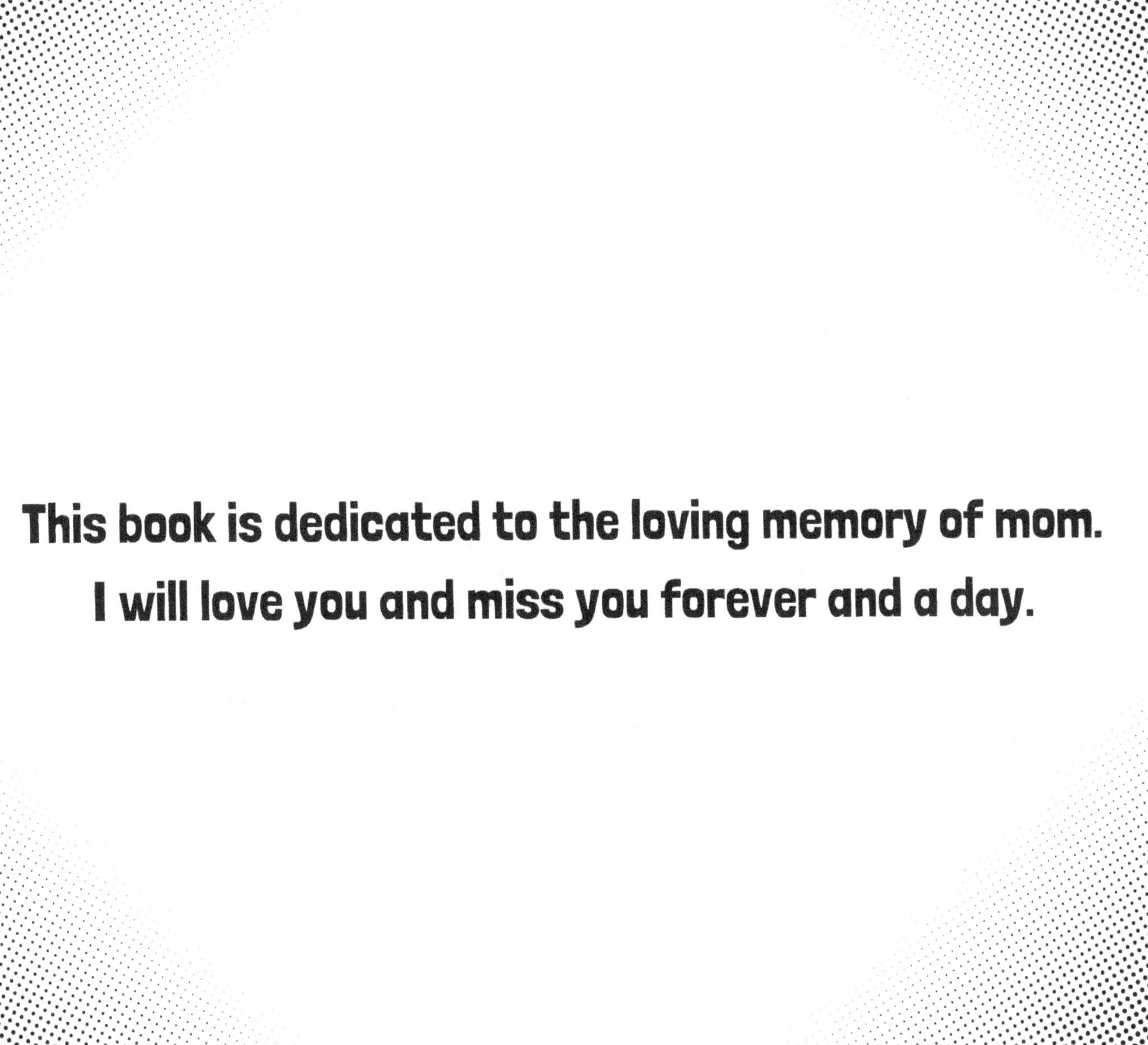
This book is dedicated to the loving memory of mom.
I will love you and miss you forever and a day.

A

is for
ALL the housework.

2

B

**is for
your aching BACK.**

AAAUGH!
SNAP
!

C

is for

CLIPPING the toe nails.

D
is for

What is DROPPED on the floor.

8

E is for

EXERCISES you help them do while hurting yourself.

10

F

is for

the FUN moments you can still share.

PooF
BREAD FLOUR
RECIPES

G

is for

just needing to GET out

once in a while.

14

H

is for

HARPING on them to be careful.

I

is for

INSURANCE and the mountain of bills.

18

J
is for
expecting to JUMP
when they call.

K

is for remaining KIND to others when dealing with your own challenges.

FOR Carolyn
For Jan
For Donna

L is for
LOTION and those
ewwwww moments.

Skin Lotion

M

is for

keeping track of their

MEDICATIONS.

26

N

is for

those NAKED parts that

shouldn't be seen....

by anybody!

28

O

O is for

frequent and ongoing doctor OFFICE visits.

P

is for

PEE PADS and

hoping nobody notices.

Not for me.
Nothing I to see here.
Not for me...
Pee Pads
Pee Pads
Pee Pads
Pee Pads

32

Q is for

being repeatedly asked the same QUESTIONS.

R

is for
feeling like you're
RUNNING on empty.

E
F
To Do

S

S is for needing to change the STINKY diapers.

T

is for

TOUGH LOVE when feelings

are fractured.

U

is for

trying to rub out URINE

stains from the carpet.

42

V

is for welcomed VISITS from friends.

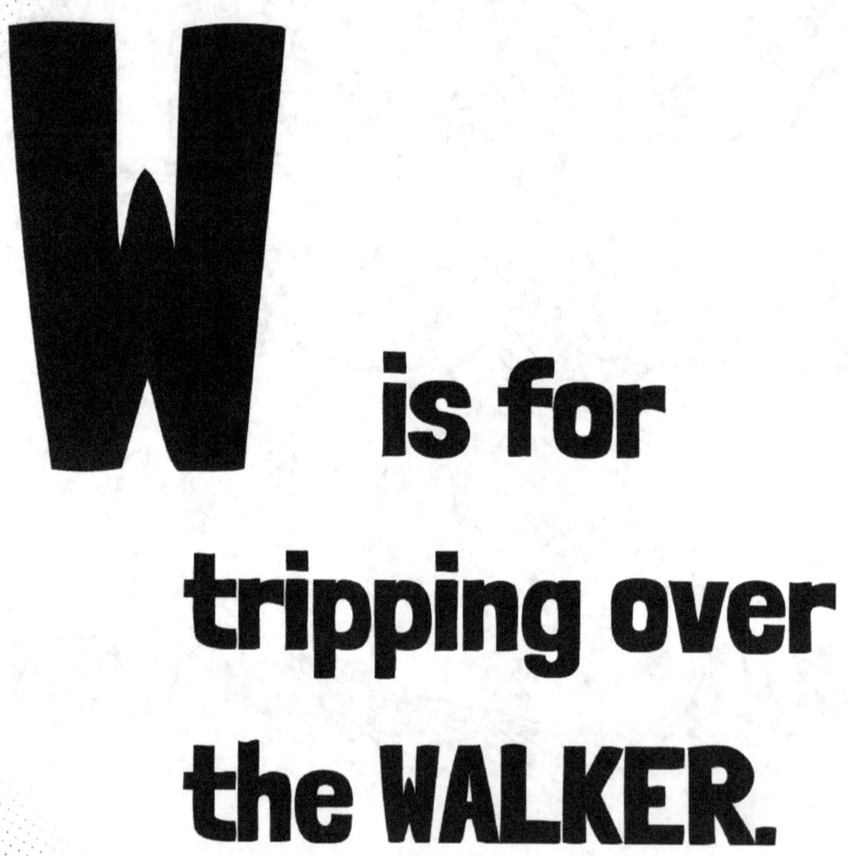

W
is for
tripping over
the WALKER.

46

X is for

how many TIMES you get mad at each other but make up just as quickly.

BLAAAH!
Well, BLAAAH! to you too!

Y

is for

a daily reminder that you're not as YOUNG as you used to be.

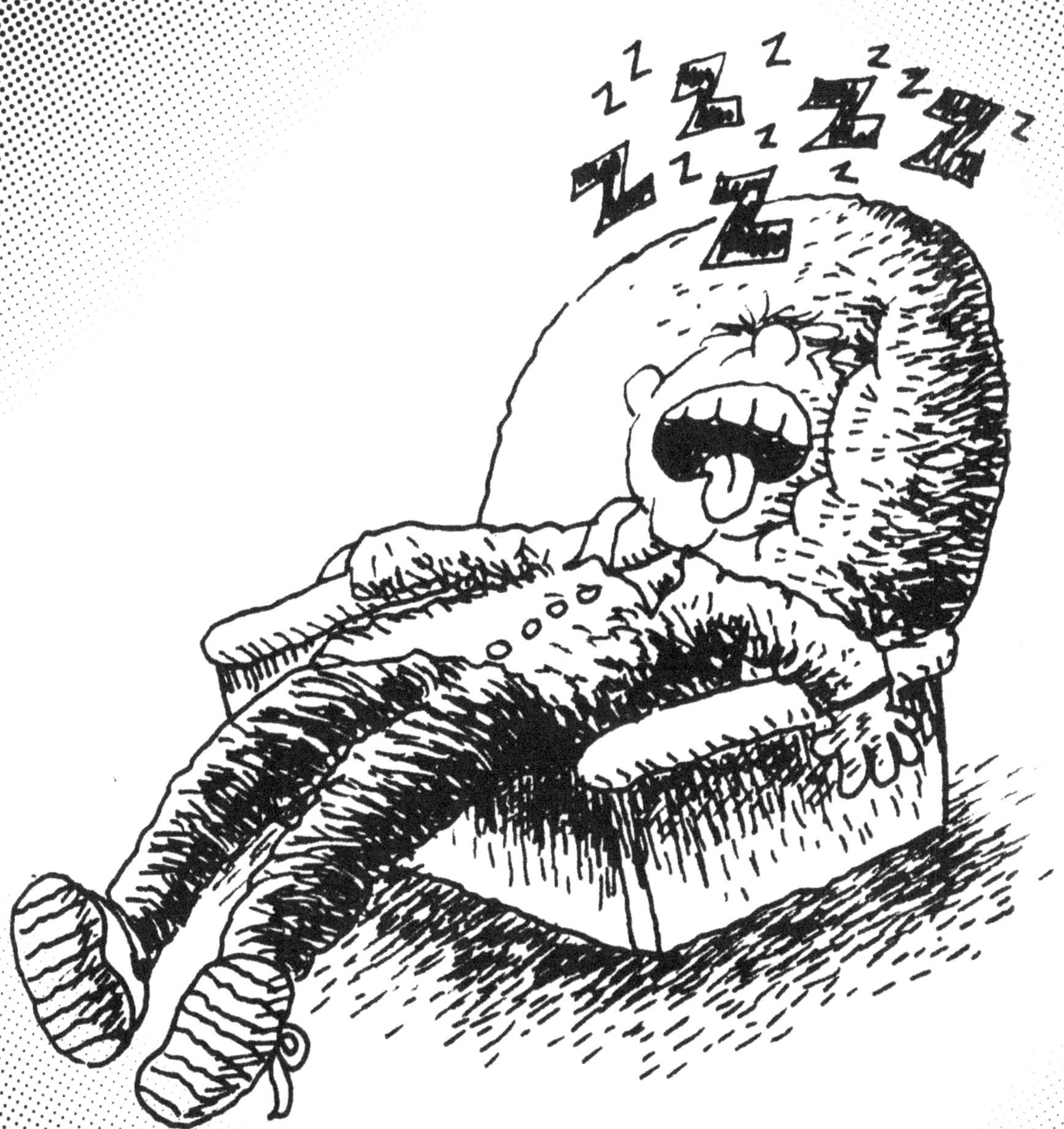

Z

Z

Z is for your love for them being a ZILLION times a ZILLION.

Mr. Ollie attended art school and launched his career in ad agencies, where he self-syndicated editorial cartoons to 25 newspapers in Tennessee. Since 1987, he has served as a "teaching artist," traveling to schools across the southeastern U.S. and beyond through state and local art agencies. He has been honored with the Outstanding Artist in Residence Award from the Tennessee Arts Commission and the School Bell Award from the Tennessee Education Association for his work on educational issues. A long-time member of the National Cartoonists Society, Mr. Ollie resides on a twelve-acre farm in Lewisburg, Tennessee. His cartoons and illustrations have been featured in numerous publications, including The Saturday Evening Post, Woman's World, Boy's Life, The American Legion Magazine, Ebony, Mature Years, Highlights for Children, Cobblestone, Dig, Odyssey, Appleseeds, and many others.

9 7 9 8 3 3 0 4 9 2 5 0 3